I0213508

HOLY
CHUTZPAH

HOLY
CHUTZPAH

Walking in
Godly Boldness

Annette M. Eckart

Bridge for Peace Publishers

Wading River, New York

Bridge for Peace Publishers
Wading River, New York

First Printing, June 2013

Holy Chutzpah: Walking in Godly Boldness
Copyright © 2012 Annette M. Eckart
ISBN 978-0-9845306-1-8

Available at Bridge for Peace Publishers
PO Box 789, Wading River, NY 11792
Phone (631) 730-3982 fax (631) 730-3995
www.bridgeforpeace.org

All rights reserved.
No part of this publication may be reproduced or transmitted in any form or by any means, electronic or mechanical, including photocopying, recording, or any information storage or retrieval system, without prior permission in writing from the publisher.

Scriptures in this book include direct quotations, as well as the author's adaptations, from various translations of the Holy Bible.

Printed in U.S.A.

Holy Chutzpah
Walking in Godly Boldness

Table of Contents

Preface

"Have I not told you: be strong and stand firm?
Be fearless and undaunted, for go where you may,
Yahweh your God is with you."
                                                    – Joshua 1:9

Enjoy *Holy Chutzpah*
and benefit from the stories

Holy Chutzpah took shape as I immersed myself in
Scripture—it's the only way I know how to read the
Bible. The Holy Spirit inspired the scriptural Word.
Sometimes the writer records events like an artist
painting a detailed picture. Particulars of the scene
are noted, as in passages about the building of the
temple. Specific materials and precise measurements,
various colors and exact weights to be used in the
building of the temple and its interior decoration are

i

preserved in the record for us to read. We imagine, or some have even recreated in pictures or sculpture, what the temple looked like based on those details. At other times, scriptural passages are sketchy like quick pencil drawings. They invite the reader to explore further. The passage says to me, "Well? Are you really interested?" I can leave the simple words there on the page or take them into prayer, letting them roll through my God-given imaginative mind, and, with some study of the historical period and societal customs of the era, let the Holy Spirit inspire me to enter the story.

Envisioning myself there, I prayerfully imagine the unfolding of the scriptural narrative by meditating on what the biblical character may have thought or felt. During meditation on the passage I consider the dialogue between men and women, the private thoughts of a prophet, and the feelings in the hearts of those portrayed. *Holy Chutzpah* is the result of my meditations.

As I read and reread the scriptural stories, the settings and cultures have become a part of my own history. The characters and their life stories are etched in my own heart. The result has been an intimate relationship with those who have gone before me.

I consider the scriptural stories to be my own history, as though I personally passed through the Red Sea to the Promised Land. (Exodus 14) I imagine their feelings and thoughts, even as I imagine what my own relatives who traveled the Atlantic to come to America experienced. These are the nature of the reflections I offer here. They are based on the Bible, some conversations are directly quoted from the Scriptures, others are biblical fiction.

I encourage you to read the Scripture reference to know exactly what the Bible says, but also to enter into the story through prayerful reflection. Immerse yourself in the living waters of the inspired word of God. As you consider the stories and their relationship to your own experiences, I pray you'll receive the blessing of *holy chutzpah* and be strengthened to walk in God's holy boldness.

Introduction

Outrageous Holiness

Chutzpah. *Hoots'-pah*! Pronounce it with extra umph on the first syllable, because *chutzpah* is an excessive kind of word. *Chutzpah* sounds like what it means—gutsy, even to the point of becoming offensive. I define *holy chutzpah* as sanctified boldness, God-fearing daring, heaven-born nerves of steel, all *holy chutzpah* qualities. And yes, a glorious gutsiness that is offensive to the enemy of our souls.

I asked my linguist friend Dr. Daniel Shapiro, "How would you describe *chutzpah*?"

"Audacity to the nth degree." Dr. Dan grew up in a Jewish area of New York where neighbors chat in Yiddish and *chutzpah* is a common word. He also speaks fluent Hebrew, Italian (earned his medical degree in Italy), Spanish, and French.

"*Chutzpah* is in popular English usage," Dr. Dan said. "You'll find it in Webster's." The dictionary defines *chutzpah* as shameless audacity, impudence, brass.

The Hebrew/Yiddish word *chutzpah* does not appear in the Bible. Yet, *holy chutzpah* is a biblical theme.

Chutzpah is often the reason an individual's experiences were recorded in the Bible. No guts, no story.

Not all stories recount *holy chutzpah*. Hellish *chutzpah* scorched a path through history. The acrid smell of destructive fires still fills our nostrils. Hellish *chutzpah* boasts of many conquests, compelling its devotees to plunder the depths of depravity and brag of their wicked exploits.

Dr. Dan recited an example of hellish *chutzpah*: "A child kills both of his parents. There's a murder trial. He pleads for mercy from the judge because he's an orphan."

In contrast to hellish *chutzpah*, every Christian conversion story smacks of *holy chutzpah*. When I was a hopeless sinner, Jesus Christ, God's only Son, submitted to gruesome execution by crucifixion to commute my sentence. Jesus was murdered. He died in my place. I had the brass to ask His Father for mercy!

Who could have convinced me of the possibility of forgiveness? My audacity must have come from the Holy Spirit. My mercy plea became the first glimmer of *holy chutzpah* in my life.

Introduction

When I stood before God the Father as my judge, God the Son defended me, served as my trial lawyer, advocated for me. Jesus exemplified outrageous love. He demonstrated audacious generosity. *Holy chutzpah*!

The Father granted my request. God forgave me because His Son took my punishment. Because Jesus bled, I went free. He died and I was adopted into a new heavenly family. I received an inheritance that included restoration to God's family and eternal life.

God's children inherit grace to imitate Jesus, to live *holy chutzpah*, a power demonstrated by others before us. David unleashed *holy chutzpah* in worship. Esther summoned *holy chutzpah* to wait. Debra discovered *holy chutzpah* to go; Ruth found enough to stay.

Enough inspiration for our lifetime overflows in the stories of biblical heroes, but let's not disqualify ourselves by assuming all *holy chutzpah* people acquire fame. The local newspaper may never highlight our story. The crucial question is: Has Jesus inscribed your name across a page in the Lamb's Book of Life? We are proud to serve boldly in obscurity, as did our Master before us.

People who advance the kingdom of God live *holy chutzpah* with daring kindness, radical forgiveness, and unflinching generosity that is not motivated by monetary surplus, but by *holy chutzpah*. They willingly pay the price to serve people both in their own neighborhoods and on the other side of the world. Some go to those whom they have never seen, motivated by a word from God. Others pray for and give to those they will never see this side of heaven, because of divine love. And still, hellish *chutzpah* gets the most press. Loud, offensive people grab the spotlight. Disrespect in families, neglected responsibilities, apathy in the workplace are widely televised. Compromise, immorality, and regret (I'm sorry you caught me) replace repentance. These issues demand a response of extreme Christian love. Inexhaustible love requires *holy chutzpah*.

We need a resurgence of *holy chutzpah*. We must find the courage through the Holy Spirit to live outrageous holy boldness in our culture.

Grab hold of godly lessons; learn secrets others discovered. Realize hidden capacities, release latent talents. Tap into the holy audacity that can remold our relationships and our world. Adventure awaits.

Holy chutzpah—God created *you* to be audacious!

Glorious
New Beginning

"I made four New Year's resolutions last night, and by twelve o'clock today I had already broken three of them!" The co-hosts laughed and I clicked off the radio.

It doesn't have to be that way. God has more than that in mind for you.

As years progress, life's disappointments and defeats cause some to lower their expectations. Cynicism develops and jaded attitudes rob joy. "Same old, same old," people mutter.

Yet, I hear a whisper in my spirit, "In the beginning God created the heavens and the earth."(Genesis 1:1)

God stretched out His arm, extended His hand, and the heavens flew from His fingers. God opened His mouth and the earth spun forth.

God created palm trees for desert spaces, their long fronds remaining green even through drought, their thirsty roots burrowing into the earth. For colder regions He formed deciduous maples—shedding their leaves in autumn, slowing their growth to survive freezing winters.

God conceived us in His mind. Created us in the perfect moment. God shaped us to thrive and overcome obstacles in a foreign land, this alien earthly home, until He calls us to Himself for all eternity.

Eye color, curly hair or straight, emotional and mental capacities—all designed by God with purpose. Nothing left to chance. But we need *holy chutzpah* in order to live God's plan.

To equip us for the task, he fortified our hearts with a spark of *holy chutzpah*. (Proverbs 28:1, Ephesians 6:20)

Holy chutzpah—sacred audacity to the nth degree, blessed boldness. *Holy chutzpah*—staying power under pressure, tenacity when it hurts to hold on.

Jesus demonstrated qualities of *holy chutzpah* when He humbled himself and became human, loved the unlovable, confronted corruption, stood silent before His accusers, and said "yes" to His Father in the Garden of Gethsemane where He shuddered at the ordeals to come.

In the beginning, God created us to be like Jesus.

Self-made resolutions will never satisfy us. We need daily transformation, becoming new creations through the blood of Jesus Christ. God invites us to travel a wondrous road with Him.

Grab hold of *holy chutzpah*; let's begin the journey. A new expedition—immersing ourselves in God's Word and meeting bold saints who have passed this way. God created us to be audacious!

※

Eternal God, You designed me to be daring for You. Yet I tremble to begin something new, asking, "What if I embarrass myself or if I fail? What will people say?"
Help me to pose new questions. "How can I serve You with Holy Chutzpah *today, Lord? Who needs a blessing today, Father? Will You please show me how to help? May I be Your messenger?"*
In the beginning, You created me with Holy Chutzpah. *(Romans 8:15) Enliven me again with a blessed boldness that will glorify Your name throughout the earth. Amen.*

Journeying

Friends lent us their twenty-two foot RV. My husband Ed and I drove the vehicle fifteen miles to a Long Island barrier beach. Both locals and visitors from other states coveted a spot in the campground because of the location. The sand spit jutted out between the Atlantic Ocean and the Great South Bay. Shades of aquamarine, turquoise, and navy blue colored the sky and the water. Fortunately, minimal midweek occupancy in the state recreation facility gave us our choice of spaces.

We parked on a rise close to the bay that lapped at the shore. Cattails rustled in the breeze. Fleets of dragonflies flew by; we heard their wings humming as they passed. At night the sound of the Atlantic Ocean crashing on the other side of the dunes filled our bedroom. I watched sparkling constellations move across the black sky.

Two days later the park began to fill as the week-end approached. Some brought satellite dishes, others Frank Sinatra recordings, and by the afternoon the place sounded like the battle of the bands. Televisions and CD players drowned out sounds of ebbing waters and crackling campfires. Many had traveled to the shore, but few had left home. They brought their mindset with them.

Some people move from here to there, but never leave. Change challenges us as it has confronted godly people before us. Include Abraham (Abram until God renamed him) in the list. Scripture says, "Then the Lord told Abram, 'Leave your country, relatives, and your father's house, and go to the land that I will show you.'" (Genesis 12:1)

Abram left, but took his relatives with him and carried his father Terah's mindset. Terah worshiped idols. (Genesis 11:31, Joshua 24:2) God prompted Abram to leave his father's ways. Abram had to find God's path.

"Leave," the Lord commands. Though my feet may follow, what tapes replay in my head? Walking into silence to discover the new requires a willingness to trust, to hope. I need *holy chutzpah* to navigate the path.

Today, I will leave behind excess noise and listen to Your voice. I trust I will hear Your counsel directing my journey to a new place in You. Thank You for supplying Holy Spirit courage that empowers me to leave on a journey with You. Amen.

New Birth
Announcement

The lanky Chinese man startled me with his unusual request. He approached Ed, my brother Kevin and me in a Xixiang market, and introduced himself as David. "May I walk with you?" the young man asked.

We strolled the ancient city's cobbled streets, smells of roasting meat drifting on the warm night air. Festive music played in the distance.

"Did you know there once was a King David?" David shook his head no. "He was a man who loved God!" Kevin developed his theme, dramatically emphasizing King David's story, speaking about the monarch as though he had personally known him. David listened intently, nodding and asking Kevin questions as he recounted the ancient Scriptures.

The next day, Ed and I returned to the marketplace. Unexpectedly, David fell into step alongside us. This time, I spoke of the Holy Spirit. "Jesus sent the Spirit to teach us all things." (John 14:26) David had heard of Jesus, but never about the Spirit. He wanted to receive the Holy Spirit. We prayed.

"Everything looks different," he exclaimed. "I am different. I will never be the same. This is the most important day of my life!"

The next day, we flew south to distant Kunming. Two days later David telephoned. "I am in Kunming on business. Can we get together?" After making arrangements with David, Ed contacted local missionaries who supplied him with a Bible in David's language.

We met on a street corner. David didn't have much time. Ed discreetly handed him the Bible. David crossed the ten-lane road and hailed a taxi. He turned to us, grinning and waving before climbing into the car.

I whispered, "We have our first Chinese son."

Ed was fifty-four, I was turning fifty. Abraham was seventy-five, his wife sixty-five, when he heard God's remarkable promise. "This is My covenant with you, I will make you the father of not just one nation but of a multitude of nations!" (Genesis 17:4) God's promise seemed impossible, but bold Abraham believed.

Jesus taught that everyone must be reborn. (John 3:3) We need *holy chutzpah* to bring forth spiritual children for God's kingdom.

Holy Spirit, I want to become a spiritual parent to a great many people. Abraham believed You and became a father to many nations. Use me to bring Your precious rebirth to others all over the world. Arrange divine appointments for me. I want to witness the rebirth of many for Your glory. Amen.

Relentless
Holy Chutzpah

I wish you could meet my friend Gus Schuck, a real *holy chutzpah* man. Jewish from birth, he anguished over the reality of Jesus, the God of his wife Gloria. He begged Jehovah to show him truth. Revelation broke through. Baptism followed. Gus is a Christian who burns to be a blessing.

Gus, a grandparent on the verge of retirement, worked as a supermarket checker. Gloria was employed as a secretary. He suffered with Hodgkin's lymphoma. Gloria endured diabetes and a heart attack. She underwent quadruple bypass surgery. Despite these challenges, Gus had the holy audacity to imagine they could throw Jesus an enormous interdenominational birthday party for the year 2000.

"It'll be a huge birthday celebration," he said, waving his arms. "We'll invite everybody. We'll hold it at the Nassau Coliseum." The indoor arena seats 18,300.

Ed and I believed in the vision and accepted Gus and Gloria's invitation to join the Executive Board.

The date drew close. A generous friend of the Schucks had donated the ten thousand dollar down payment to reserve the stadium, but we had little money for the large balance due on the Coliseum, not to mention the cost of insurance, sound systems, and other needs.

Tension brewed among the Board members. A man raised his voice at a meeting, "Plan A is unattainable. I suggest we go to plan B, a smaller venue."

Gus shot back, "Only the Nassau Coliseum will do! This is a birthday party for *Jesus Christ!*" He was relentless. The Schucks doubled their efforts. God blessed their labors and the money came in.

On the day of the event, we arrived very early at the venue because Ed was in charge of all arrangements for the day. Scores of volunteers reported for their assignments. Twelve thousand people celebrated Jesus for a glorious three hours. The arena buzzed with stories of reconciliations and reunions, renewed hope and recommitments to Jesus Christ.

After the crowd went home, the house lights went up. Ed's walkie-talkie had crackled with men's questions for eleven hours, but now it was silent. We sat in the empty stands and held hands. I thanked God for Gus and Gloria's passionate chutzpah to be a blessing.

"I will bless you, and I will make you a blessing to others." (Genesis 12:2b)

God inspired Abraham to move forward with these words. Abraham knew tensions, discord, and unrest. He must have known the temptation to abandon God's vision. How often did he steel himself with *holy chutzpah*, recalling the promise, rehearsing the words until they became his reality? Abraham held to God's promise and pushed through to his goal.

※

Lord, I want to be relentless for You. Bless me with Holy Chutzpah, *so that I may believe for Your best. Amen.*

A Name Change

"I've never met anyone named Sunday before," I said as we exited the commercial building in New York City. Victor, our African missionary-friend, had introduced us to Sunday, his countryman who worked there.

Victor laughed, "In our country, some families name their first-born Sunday. The subsequent children would be named Monday, Tuesday and so on through the week. It doesn't matter what day of the week they are actually born on, the days indicate their birth order. Christians don't follow that tradition."

Peter, another missionary, said, "The eighth child will be named Blank. If they have more children, parents call them Blank-One, Blank-Two, and so forth." The African men chuckled.

I was horrified. *Sticks and stones can break my bones and names* can *hurt.*

Six months later, Mark Excel, a Nigerian missionary, visited us. "My father was a pastor. He knew the value of a name. He called me Excel and I intend to live up to it. I have named my son Gospel."

Gospel means good news, how beautiful. The boy will know God chose him as a special messenger, that he is good news.

God values names. He commanded Zechariah to name his son John. (Luke 1:13) He told Mary to call her son Jesus. (Luke 1:31)

God also renames people for his prophetic purposes. (Genesis 17:5 and 15, Genesis 32:28) He spoke to Abram saying, "…I'm changing your name… It will no longer be Abram; now you will be known as Abraham, for you will be the father of many nations." "Abram" means "exalted father"; "Abraham" means "father of many." The new name promised Abraham a promotion!

Holy chutzpah helped Abraham to believe God renamed him to indicate his destiny. Accepting his new name demonstrated his belief in his God-given future. Abraham must have said to himself, "I'm not going to answer to that old name anymore. I will be the father of many, and I'm going to start answering to Abraham and nothing else." Do you think Abraham knew that how he thought of himself was more important than what anyone else called him? The day Abraham started to call himself "father of many," he stepped into God's vision for his life. When he began to introduce himself as "father of many" he announced his destiny.

❦

Lord, breathe into my heart Your special name for me and I will answer to no other. Amen.

God's Friend

Her marriage was in trouble. They planned to separate. She called me to pray with her on the phone. Compassion filled my heart. I grieved for their marriage. After releasing the Blood of Jesus into their situation, I heard God speak to me.

Pray to Me as your friend.

I had never addressed God publicly as "friend" before. I had limited that aspect of our relationship to my private devotions. Though I felt uneasy, I obeyed and continued to pray openly.

"Father, You created the family. I know Your heart is turned toward the family. I know You desire to see all marriages whole and holy. Lord, as Your friend, I would consider it a special favor to me to see this marriage restored."

God wanted to hear me pray in that particular way. Not as a friend of the caller, but as His friend.

The next day, she called again. "Last night we had a breakthrough. I saw a real change of heart. We have a starting place and we're committed to working it out."

I thanked the Holy Spirit who gave me courage to pray as God instructed me, as God's friend.

Abraham knew God as friend. (2Chronicles 20:7) God revealed truths to Abraham because of their special relationship. Prudent people do not share everything with everyone. Neither does the Lord. He chooses His confidants; Abraham was one of them. "'Should I hide my plan from Abraham?' the Lord asked." (Genesis 18:17)

Abraham knew his own condition, describing himself as "dust and ashes." (Genesis 18:27b) He also knew God treasured him. That knowledge freed Abraham to pray with *holy chutzpah,* a boldness that pleased God. His position as God's friend did not foster arrogance, but resulted in a heart of mercy. A heart like God's. Through Abraham's intercession three lives were spared from destruction. (Genesis 19:16-26)

❧

Lord, teach me to become a better friend to You, like Your confidant, Abraham. He persevered in prayer, and You rescued three people. Your desire is that none should perish. (2Peter 3:9) Inspire me to bold intercession. Amen.

Ordinary Day, Extraordinary Possibilities

"Where to first, Lord? The gas station or the supermarket?" *The supermarket.* "Okay."

Thinking over the best route to the nearest store as I drove up the main road, I passed the gas station. I had locked my Honda and was looking for a cart in the huge parking lot when I saw Peggy.

"It's been so long," we said, exchanging hugs.

"I don't think it's an accident that we're meeting," Peggy said. She told me that her family would commemorate the one-year anniversary of her father John's death with a memorial service that morning.

"It's a rough day," Peggy said.

I nodded, remembering moments of prayer I had shared with John on the phone as he struggled with cancer's debilitating effects. He impressed me as gentle and faith-filled. "Peggy, let's pray," I said. Standing in the parking lot, we joined hands, thanked

God for eternal life, and asked for comfort. "Lord, may they remember good times today and find their strength in You."

Peggy said she felt ready for the day, and I felt grateful. Later, I remembered my simple prayer, "Where to...?" God had turned an ordinary shopping experience into something special.

God's fingerprints often appear in the routine, creating the remarkable. We trace the pattern back to Genesis, where the writer records an everyday scene.

"It was evening and the women were coming out to draw water." (Genesis 24:11) The scorching sun began to set, the air cooled and, for the second time that day, women strolled out of their village to collect necessary water. Rebekah walked the mile with them.

Meanwhile, the patriarch Abraham sent his trusted servant Eliezer to Aram-Naharaim to find a wife for his son Isaac from Abraham's own people. Eliezer had just arrived at Rebekah's village when the women appeared with their water jugs. He began to pray for his assignment's success. Because of his prayer, Rebekah's everyday journey to provide for her family's needs had an astonishing outcome. She impressed Eliezer and he suggested she wed his master's son. Rebekah accepted the proposal, married Isaac, and their progeny appear in the genealogy of Jesus. I imagine when Rebekah started out for the well that morning it looked like just another ordinary day.

Lord, I often feel pressured, rushing to complete daily chores. Meanwhile, You plan to act in my day's ordinary details. Help me develop praying chutzpah! I want to live today in expectation of Your presence in the humdrum. I will sing a song of praise and transform menial jobs into worship by seeking Your help. When I approach ordinary tasks with prayer, they hold extraordinary possibilities. Amen.

Holy Chutzpah Hospitality

On a trip to the Middle East in 1991, my husband and I attended several days of a lavish wedding ceremony that continued for two weeks. One afternoon, on the flat roof of the bride's home, I sat surrounded by two-dozen young ladies in sumptuous attire reminiscent of *Arabian Nights* — sheer veils, gold bangle bracelets, and dangling earrings.

The girls appointed a striking young woman named Arie as their spokesperson and she drew up a folding chair alongside me. Arie demonstrated both maturity and grace while translating the group's questions and quizzing me in broken English. A little farther away, the others whispered and giggled behind their jeweled fingers. These privileged young ladies also had the benefit of learning English in their private schools, but only Arie had the *holy chutzpah* to utilize what she knew.

My husband's approaching footsteps on the stairs alarmed the young women. Like a flock of birds taking to the air, they jumped up and fluttered off, veils flapping behind them. Though my husband was an invited guest, their society discouraged young unmarried ladies from speaking with unrelated men.

Their superb hospitality and cultural rules have a long history. Unmarried middle eastern women avoided men in general and male strangers in particular. Yet, thousands of years ago, when a thirsty traveler approached lovely Rebekah—a decisive woman with a ready heart—she responded generously to his request for a drink. "'Certainly, sir,' she said, and she quickly lowered the jug for him to drink." (Genesis 24:18)

How common was it for a young woman to speak to a stranger at the well? Certainly, as a single woman, it would be imprudent to allow an outsider to come close enough to drink from her jug. Yet, God inspired Rebekah to do the unusual. Because she yielded to *holy chutzpah*, God blessed her with a great reward. She distinguished herself in the eyes of God and Eliezer through her bold service and married a tribal prince–Isaac.

Holy Chutzpah Hospitality

~❧~

Lord, our society often shuns people with illnesses and disabilities. Frequently, elderly and materially poor people find themselves devalued. They thirst. Will I allow them to come close enough to drink?

When a shy person stands awkwardly at the gathering let me be the first to offer hospitality. When a frustrated supermarket clerk needs a kind word, I want to speak with Holy Chutzpah. *Stir me to serve the stranger I meet by easing the moment with Your graciousness. May I offer Your living water to thirsty strangers. Amen.*

Enthusiastic Service

Renae and her mother Sharron sat at the table enjoying a "cuppa" (Australian for a cup of coffee) on their 500 acre farm. Sheep grazed in the fields and turkeys trilled their God-given song, their gravelly voices running up the musical scale. *Crickle-crackle, crickle-crackle.* Renae's ears perked up. "What's that sound, Mom?"

The women flung open the front door to investigate.

"Whoa!" Renea exclaimed. Flames shot from the passenger seat of their utility truck. Renae ran for the hose. Fearing the truck would explode, Sharron dialed the bushfire brigade. Renae unknotted the hose line while her mother grabbed a bucket and filled it. They met at the fire and Sharron yelled, "Get back Renae, I can afford to die!" Renae shook her head and hauled the hose to the site.

The women could have watched from the safety of the house until help arrived, but instead they flung water on the blaze fighting with all their might never realizing a blessing was in store.

A handsome young fireman who responded to the emergency call admired Renae's spunk—and more. In a matter of months he asked Renae to marry him and they are living happily ever after!

Rebekah also found a husband by responding wholeheartedly to a need.

Eliezer drank the refreshment Rebekah offered. "When he had finished she said, 'I'll draw water for your camels, too, until they have had enough!'" (Genesis 24:19)

Though Rebekah shouldered a weighty watering pot, she volunteered to fetch cool well-water for the stranger's ten camels. Each camel could drink up to twenty-five gallons. Since a gallon of water weighs approximately eight pounds, Rebekah offered to lug over two hundred pounds of water per camel. Multiplied by ten camels, that equals two thousand pounds—literally a ton of water!

Other women had come out from the village to draw at the well. Rebekah didn't compare her workload with theirs. She saw the need, knew her ability, and eagerly set to work. She could have handed the jug to the camel-owner, but she enjoyed testing her strength to be a blessing.

Rebekah built her stamina to the point of confidently hauling a ton of water. When she had a literal ton of water to move she set to work methodically and with enthusiasm. That's *holy chutzpah*! Read on to the end of the Genesis story and you'll find Eliezer prayed for a young woman to respond with enthusiasm. Rebekah's willingness won her a husband and a place in the lineage of Jesus Christ.

～❧～

Lord, today I ask boldness to enthusiastically embrace the tasks You put before me. I will happily exert myself on behalf of others. Give me Rebekah's delight in my labors, especially when I seem to have a ton of work. Amen.

Inspired Speech

After months of study I scheduled the federal licensing exam in Manhattan. Immediately after I'd completed the process the computer would calculate my score. My career depended on the outcome. On my way to catch the city-bound train, I rushed into the drug store. Tension pounded in my temples while I dug into my purse to pay the pharmacist.

"Relax," he said in a kindly tone, "you have all the time you need."

Surprised, I looked up. God had reassured me with a sign of His presence through the druggist. Immediately, my stress level dropped. Hugging the words to myself, I left the shop. The storeowner probably thought he was just being friendly, but the Spirit had inspired his words.

Sometimes, God amazes me with reminders of His intimate involvement in my life. At other times, I wait and watch expecting Him to act in answer to my prayer. Eliezer asked God for a sign and waited by a well for his answer.

Eliezer prayed, "If she says, 'Yes, certainly, and I will water your camels, too!'—let her be the one You have appointed as Isaac's wife. By this I will know that You have shown kindness to my master." (Genesis 24:14b)

While the village women clustered around the well chatting, Rebekah spoke to the stranger. She offered to tend Eliezer's animals.

Rebekah thought watering Eliezer's camels was her own good idea. She did not know he had requested a sign. Rebekah's idea was *God's* idea; her words originated with the Holy Spirit—they were God's sign to Eliezer. Her conversation was significant.

Holy Spirit, You call us to speak for You. Words tumble from my mouth all day long. Small-talk floods the world. When I hear You nudge me—speak to that person—sometimes my mouth goes dry. I hesitate over God-inspired words. Later, I condemn myself for missed opportunities, creating more anxiety that will surface the next time You prompt me. Holy Spirit, You guided the pharmacist and Rebekah, they were unaware of their messenger roles. Help me to relax and know that as I submit my speech to You, You will speak through me. Amen.

Facing Fears

"You need to sit down together and look at your finances," I counseled Barb. The couple's debt strained their relationship. Ignoring her husband's warnings, she continued to overspend. He worried, wrote checks, and blamed her. They had a load to carry together but Barb feared the required changes that would bring fiscal sanity.

Thankfully, Barb yielded to a weekly financial meeting designed to assess their situation. It took *holy chutzpah* to return to the table time and again, and to labor through bills and budgets.

In time, Barb overcame her fears. She grew strong, trimmed spending, and learned to live within her means. She finds monitoring household finances hard work, but she also finds satisfaction in mastering a budget. She discovered hidden capabilities and increased marital harmony. Encouraged by her successes, Barb has become enthusiastic about administrating her household expenses.

People who face a challenge with an eager heart inspire me. Rebekah was such a woman. The Word says,"...she quickly emptied the jug into the watering trough and ran down to the well again." (Genesis 24:20)

Rebekah, strong and enterprising, moved with enthusiasm, bent quickly, watched the water slosh into the trough, and ran back to the community well with her empty jug. Rebekah would have attached the vessel to a rope, lowered it into the spring, and hauled the heavy jar up. She was agile—though the work was cumbersome. Rebekah's job sounds easy in this passage because she had mastered the work. Rebekah built her stamina to the point of confidently hauling a ton of water. She strengthened herself over time and then used her gift to help others.

❧

Holy Spirit, how often do I grumble and hang back, ignoring the work before me? How much energy do I spend in procrastination? Do I allow fear to dominate areas of my life? Thank You for people who show me I can learn to overcome my apprehensions. Release Holy Chutzpah *within me, I want Rebekah's remarkable zeal. Amen.*

Secret Joy

"I don't know why I ever started this project," Stella, a nursing home volunteer under my supervision, complained. "No one appreciates me."

I had walked down the hallway in time to hear her remark.

Two staff members behind the nurses' desk looked the other way. One rolled her eyes at me. Because Stella made an issue out of every little service she performed, no one wanted to deal with her any longer.

"Isn't there someone around who can help me?" Stella persisted.

"I thought you were here to help us," one employee retorted.

Stella resented the candor. She spun around to face me and blustered, "I resign as of this moment!"

Some people demand accolades, always drawing attention to themselves. Others scheme to scrape by with the least amount of work possible. Rebekah demonstrated generosity in service. A *holy chutzpah* woman, Rebekah found pleasure in blessing others, even though it required extra effort on her part.

When Rebekah first began to carry water for the camels she sprinted from the trough to the well. She felt energetic and glad to help someone in need. However, after several round trips, she broke into a sweat while hoisting the heavy vessel. She emptied and refilled her jug time and again while the owner of the caravan stood silently watching. "She kept carrying the water to the camels until they had finished drinking." (Genesis 24:20b)

No one lifted a finger to help.

When the sun touched the horizon, painting clouds with flaming color, the other women raised brimming water pots to their shoulders, chores completed. They leisurely walked back to the village. Talking easily among themselves, they anticipated a relaxed evening meal with family.

Rebekah, involved in her work, seemed not to notice others were returning home. She had offered her services. Though Rebekah was tiring, she would complete the job.

Jesus, alert me to ways I can help without anyone knowing. Give me holy assignments and let them remain our little secrets. Acting as Your personal emissary yields a private pleasure that far exceeds any worldly recognition. Amen.

Personal Excellence

"I don't know what happened to Marie," Pat said. "We agreed to meet at 2:00. I waited for half an hour. No sign of her. I had to come ahead or miss the boat." She had volunteered to help serve the meal on the Bridge for Peace Sunset Praise Cruise which was set to sail in just a few moments.

Pat and I stood side-by-side dishing up the barbecued chicken and corn when Marie suddenly appeared, holding out her plate.

"Marie! I'm happy you're here," I said, placing meat on her plate. She looked overheated and a bit flustered.

"Thank you," Marie replied quietly and moved to Pat's station beside me.

"I'm glad you made it," Pat said.

"No thanks to you," Marie retorted.

"I waited until I had to leave. Where were you?" Pat asked, her concern evident.

"Where was *I*? Where were *you*?" Marie snapped, eyes flashing, face flushing darker.

Uh-oh, I thought, *storm warnings.*

"I waited for you in the parking lot. You never showed *up!*" Marie's voice grew louder with each word.

"I'm sorry, Marie. Apparently, I misunderstood. I apologize. I don't think this is the time to discuss it. May we talk about this later?" Pat asked.

I watched Pat's humble chutzpah. Admiring her, I made a mental note. One year later, Pat became our public relations manager at Bridge for Peace.

Every day, people notice behavior. Eliezer observed Rebekah. "The servant watched her in silence, wondering whether or not she was the one the Lord intended him to meet." (Genesis 24:21)

Wise Eliezer remained silent, did not disclose his objective. Was Rebekah God's choice for his master's son? Though her outer attractiveness was obvious, Eliezer was watching for signs of her inner character. He noted how she strode back and forth watering the animals, enjoying her chosen assignment, oblivious to Eliezer's scrutiny. He mentally tallied his observations, arriving at a favorable conclusion regarding Rebekah.

Lord, by Your grace I will dare to hold myself to a standard of godly excellence. I know my daily attitudes reveal my true character. While the world formulates excuses, is satisfied with the bare minimum, and settles for the easy way, help me to take responsibility for my actions and find accountability partners. Amen.

Audacious Generosity

Turkish music played while our six dinner guests ordered spicy lamb and bulgur rice dishes. We celebrated my fiftieth birthday on a Friday with my oldest friend and closest family.

The next day my aunt hosted an elegant birthday luncheon for my cousin and me. Dozens of family members filled the private room.

Driving home after Sunday church, I sighed. "This has been a perfect weekend." Ed parked in front of our ranch home.

I glanced out the window, then stared hard at the scores of people on our front lawn wearing grins and colorful conical hats with elastic bands beneath their chins.

Who are those people?

Ed opened my passenger door, his smile filled his whole face. I stepped out of the car to a chorus of "*Surprise!*"

Friends closed in around me. I felt my heart carried off on a wave of love.

Inside they had piled pretty packages on our table. All of this love and presents besides? Overwhelmed, I shook my head and hugged each dear person.

I wonder what Rebekah felt when Eliezer surprised her with lavish gifts. Genesis 24:22 says, "Then at last, when the camels had finished drinking, he gave her a gold ring for her nose and two large gold bracelets for her wrists." Imagine the scene.

"Ah, at last those thirsty ships of the desert have had their fill," Rebekah chuckles as her eyes rake over the camels. She traipses to the spring one last time, dips into the water and splashes her flaming face. She studies the contented camels and their keeper. *What a story I will have to tell tonight.*

Eliezer approaches and bows slightly. Rebekah nods in return. He reaches into the folds of his flowing garment, saying, "Please accept these gifts." When he produces several pieces of ornate gold jewelry, Rebekah catches her breath.

"Sir, the service itself brought me joy, and you would add all of this to my happiness?" The woman served without expectation of compensation, but with godly generosity.

Lord, thank You for friends who model generosity coupled with holy audacity. They give without expecting a return, finding service to be its own reward. While the world embraces a "what's in it for me" philosophy, Your people find pure pleasure in blessing others. I ask You for Holy Chutzpah in giving. Inspire me to extravagant generosity—a characteristic of Your own heart. Amen.

Holy Chutzpah to Go

We spread a detailed map of China on our coffee table. Laying hands on Shanghai and Beijing, we prayed for the nation. We continued for three years. Someday, we would go to China on mission.

Through God's intricate plan, a Chinese missionary and his American wife entered our lives. After our first meeting they surprised us with an invitation. "We're expecting you in China in May."

"That's only a few weeks away!" I said, thinking of the necessary preparations. Ed and I began to pray to know if this was God's timing.

Within days the Holy Spirit confirmed the trip. God had sent us this couple as guides. They knew the country, spoke various Chinese dialects, would manage our transportation to worship with Chinese Christians in remote areas, and would arrange for us to minister to missionaries in the city. Ed telephoned the couple, "Yes," he said, "we will go."

I call these invitations from God "the go word." The Old Testament records a passage where Rebekah had to make a decision. Would she go?

Suddenly, Eliezer had appeared in her life with an agreeable marriage proposal. Rebekah's family knew Abraham as their relative. They admired the gold jewelry he had sent. Tales of Abraham's flocks of sheep, herds of cattle, abundance of precious silver, and his fortune in prized gold had fired their imaginations. Stories of his large quantities of servants, camels, and donkeys must have convinced them that Abraham had accumulated vast wealth and wielded great influence. Isaac, the only son of Abraham, what an excellent match for Rebekah!

Yet, her family wanted to delay the young woman's departure. Eliezer objected.

"So they called Rebekah. 'Are you willing to go with this man?' they asked her.

"And she replied, 'Yes, I will go.'"
(Genesis 24:57-58)

Bold, decisive Rebekah, determined to step fearlessly into her future without delay, exemplifies *holy chutzpah*. The household must have flown into action, packing belongings, loading camels, saying goodbye. Rebekah's childhood nurse and other servants accompanied her. She mounted a camel and Eliezer's servants led the way into a new life.

Lord, even when Your best choice for me seems obvious, I still sometimes postpone decisions. Some people waiver until their uncertainties become missed opportunities. You have given me the Holy Chutzpah *Rebekah modeled. May I utilize Your gift and communicate my decisions in concise language that reflects clear thinking. When I hear from You, I want to go without hesitation. Amen.*

Homecomings

"I guess I have to go back home now." Michelle's head drooped as she studied her sneakers. Her stringy blonde hair hid her sixteen-year-old face.

Returning home was not a welcome prospect for Michelle. The court designated her as a "person in need of supervision" and mandated her placement in the live-in center. As I became familiar with Michelle's situation I concluded her parents were the ones in need of supervision. Michelle needed love, guidance, and protection–a safe environment where she could mature and develop her gifts.

"It's time," I said, nodding. In three days Michelle and four other teens in my drama/dance class would don cap and gown for graduation exercises. They all feared their family reunions.

"You think my parents will show?" she asked.

"Yes. I think they will." *Jesus, guide her. Guide all of them.*

Michelle sighed. She lifted her chin and I knew she had resolved to make a new start with her family. She chose *holy chutzpah.*

Homecoming terrifies some people. Jacob had agonized over his return home. He had coveted his older brother Esau's inheritance. Jacob connived until he laid hold of Esau's birthright. Then Jacob schemed to deceive his father Isaac. Jacob's name means "he deceives," and he played his role successfully. Having enraged his brother and grieved his father, Jacob ran far and long to a new land. He married there and raised children.

Then the Lord said to Jacob, "Return to the land of your father and grandfather and to your relatives there, and I will be with you." (Genesis 31:3)

Jacob had left on bad terms. His life in Paddan-Aram, his father-in-law's home, was no paradise, but the thought of facing his family filled him with dread. How would they receive him?

Yet, Jacob believed God. It was time.

Years of exile had changed Jacob. He experienced holy guidance in dreams. He remained true to God in an idol-worshipping land. He prepared for a probable confrontation with *holy chutzpah.* He utilized faith and intellect to create an optimal situation.

He prayed. He planned. He sent gifts ahead of him. He humbled himself before Esau.

In tense situations, Father, I want to turn to You first. When You say, "It is time," may I always seek Your detailed counsel and practical strategies for harmony in relationships before I proceed. Teach me to use faith and intellect to smooth rough paths. Through Holy Chutzpah *may You receive glory. Amen.*

Humble Holy Chutzpah

"How's the doughnut and coffee campaign going?" I asked Ed.

The firm Ed worked for also employed Hilda. Her abrasive personality grated on her coworkers' nerves, Ed's included. She was both purchasing agent and resident yeller. Everyone looked forward to her impending retirement, but Ed had decided to humble himself and befriend her.

"It's going great." Ed replied. "When I showed interest in her as a person and exercised patience, she showed me another side of her personality. We have a pleasant working relationship now. It's funny. Hilda's used to vendors taking her out for lunch and flattering her to get a sale, but she knew right away I was offering friendship, not trying to manipulate her."

"So, she's really a nice person?"

"No. She's nice to me, because I'm nice to her. She's rude to everyone else. It's still a daily battle as far as they're concerned."

A little humility goes a long way if we can find some *holy chutzpah* to practice it. Jacob learned that lesson.

After years of estrangement, he prepared to reunite with his brother Esau. Jacob sent servants ahead to deliver a conciliatory message, "Humble greetings from your servant, Jacob!" (Genesis 32:4a)

Jacob had the wisdom to know that the only course open to him was humility. Both Jacob and Esau were wealthy men with numerous servants and herds of animals. Jacob's gifts alone would not persuade his brother to forget his grievance against him and abandon his wrath. They might soften Esau's heart and momentarily placate his anger, but Esau's hot blood could easily erupt into a deadly rage.

Jacob knew only the opposite spirit would serve. He had long been an offense to Esau. Compelled to humble himself, Jacob relied on holy audacity. He threw himself at his brother's feet and hoped to be forgiven his sins. His humility moved Esau, restoring their relationship.

Holy Spirit, show me my unholy pride. How often do I wait for someone else to change, when my attitude offends You? Help me to improve a relationship today through humble chutzpah. Amen.

Honest Holy Chutzpah

"He was destitute. I'm a good Christian woman, so I took him in." The caller had watched the Bridge for Peace television program and telephoned for prayer.

I frowned while holding the receiver. *Sounds unwise.*

"Now I want him out. I've been talking embellishments."

Embellishments? What does that mean?

"When he wants me to pick him up, I've said my car won't start. How long until he figures that one out?"

She means lies!

"Have you discussed this with your pastor?" I asked.

"Oh, I go to the Holiday Church."

The Holiday Church? I searched my memory. *Maybe there's a church holding services at the local Holiday Inn.* On Sunday mornings in my neighborhood the dance club, the high school, and even the movie theater becomes a place of worship.

"Yes, I'm a member of the holiday church," the caller blithely repeated.

She means she goes to services on holidays—Christmas and Easter!

"Anyway, my problem is this: I don't want to throw him out. I'm a good Christian. I'll be the first at the pearly gates! Actually, we became intimate. If he'll divorce his wife, I'll marry him. He's bi-polar, sometimes he acts bizarre, but I doubt he'd get violent."

I was speechless. *Lord, she needs help. Where do I start?*

Self-deception. Embellishments—a pretty name for lies. Holiday church—a creative title for lack of commitment. Intimate—an elaborate word to describe an extramarital relationship. The caller had a polite name and a pleasant story for each sinful condition. Reminds me of Jacob in the Old Testament. His strong sounding masculine name meant "deceiver."

Still, when God asked Jacob his name (Genesis 32:27) he didn't dodge the question. By stating "Jacob," in effect he said, "I'm called Deceiver." In other words, "My name is Liar, Cheater, Conniver." Jacob had matured, realized his mistake, and owned his sin. He was on his way home to correct his errors.

Honest Holy Chutzpah

His honest chutzpah was the first step in a godly direction. God told him, "Your name will no longer be Jacob... It is now Israel..." (Genesis 32:28) His honesty before God brought transformation.

~❧~

Holy Spirit, guard me from the temptation to give my ugly sins pretty names. Expose areas of rationalization and self-deception. Give me the Holy Chutzpah *to be honest with myself and transparent before You. Recognition of sin and repentance are the first steps on the journey to freedom. Amen.*

Persevering
Holy Chutzpah

"Lord, I don't get it."

Rainbow prisms sparkled from the icicles outside my dormer window at the retreat center. Bare maples threw black shadows across acres of crusty white snow three stories down. I tapped my finger on the Bible passage and gazed at the wet slate roof, listening.

Every now and then I reserve a room at a quiet place, just to be present to God. I don't calendar the time to find solutions to questions. True, a tranquil day with my Counselor prepares me for life's dilemmas by tuning my ear to God's voice. But that's not why I schedule the overnight.

I need a pause in my routine to wait on God while He picks the topic of conversation, uninterrupted hours to listen for His voice.

Today, I leisurely open my Bible to notice, "...a man came and wrestled with him until dawn." (Genesis 32:24) God seems to want to talk about His wrestling match with Jacob.

"Why would you want to fight with Jacob? Why would you put Jacob's bone out of joint?"

I mulled over the story of God up close and personal with crafty Jacob. Jacob had chutzpah, plenty of it. He had the nerve to demand a blessing. Did Jacob want God's blessing in addition to what he already had without any personal cost? Or would Jacob struggle through until God transformed his impudent, audacious nature? Could Jacob's chutzpah become holy? Would Jacob place his boldness at God's service instead of self-service?

That kind of change means pain.

God wrenched Jacob's bone out of joint (*ouch*), testing his heart. Jacob stayed in the struggle demanding, "...bless me."(Genesis 32:26) God tested Jacob's boldness.

When the pressure escalated, Jacob battled through to the blessing he coveted, even though it hurt. He was willing to pay the price. He proved he was God's man.

God concluded the match. He sanctified Jacob's chutzpah and blessed a nation through him.

Father, You remind me that perseverance pleases You. I want Jacob's determination. He grabbed hold of You through the dark night until dawn broke and he received Your blessing. When the meaning of a Bible passage eludes me, let me grapple with it until You illuminate my understanding. May I not lightly skim over Your Word, but willingly engage the struggle to gain your blessing. Amen.

Tenacious
Holy Chutzpah

A piercing sound screeched through the house as missionaries from Indonesia sharpened their machetes on a grinding wheel in our garage.

"The guys are preparing for another attack on the Trees of Heaven," I thought. "That invasive species has met its match. "

The men were experienced in clearing jungles for churches and schools in their native country. Now they were teaching us to slash back the encroaching woods and weed-like trees on our vacant land. They would clear a space to raise the tent for our annual praise gathering.

Every year Trees of Heaven multiplied, advanced, and reclaimed the land. They sprang up through curb cracks. Once I saw a sapling break through an asphalt crevice and establish itself in the center of a driveway. Trees of Heaven can grow eight feet in one year.

The Trees of Heaven seem determined to take over the earth, but they had not yet met the sharp edge of machete blades wielded by single-minded Indonesian missionaries. These Christian men battled resistance in their homeland on a daily basis and had a steely determination to fill the earth with God's good news. Actually, God had told Jacob to fill the earth. "Then God said, 'I am God Almighty. Multiply and fill the earth! Become a great nation, even many nations... .'" (Genesis 35:11) If God expected Jacob to fill the earth he would have to be as unyielding as Indonesian missionaries.

Jacob had enemies. Neighboring tribes—the Canaanites and Perizzites—terrified him. He said, "We are so few that they will come and crush us. We will all be killed!" (Genesis 34:30b)

Jacob was on the run again, and he had quite a track record. He ran from his brother Esau, secretly escaped his father-in-law, and now he was making haste to Bethel.

What a relief to hear God's promise of multiplication when he had imagined extinction. Instead of shrinking back, Jacob began to advance.

Tenacious Holy Chutzpah

Lord, I know You want Your Word to multiply and Your principles to fill the earth. Train me to become increasingly proactive, rather than reactive. Make me tenacious like the Indonesian missionaries whose spirits thrive even in hostile situations. I want to be as resolute as Indonesian Christians who persist in faith in an oppressive environment. I want to flourish, especially in unlikely places. Amen.

A Living Memorial

A red rose pressed between fine white pages has marked a passage in my Bible for twelve years. The color in the petals has stained the pages, memorializing the precious times God has spoken to me through these same verses, giving instruction and understanding.

In the margin, I jotted dates and locations, recording interludes of grace. I read the entries. They recalled sweet moments of God's guidance. I remember sitting silently at the beach while waves crashed against the shore and God's word washed over me. Years later, while I bounced along in a fumy Italian bus, God deepened the meaning of these verses, affirming His direction.

Occasions of hearing God's personal word deserve special recognition. Jacob knew the importance of memorializing a God encounter. "Jacob set up a stone pillar to mark the place where God had spoken to him." (Genesis 35:14a)

A Living Memorial

As the chapter opens, God speaks to Jacob in Shechem. He instructs Jacob to return to Bethel. Jacob is to build an altar there to worship Him. After the long journey Jacob arrives and the Most High assures him that He will give the land to him and his numerous descendants. (Genesis 35:12)

God doesn't need to remind Jacob of the memorial He commanded him to build. God does not prod him saying, "Have a little chutzpah and get moving on that altar, son." Jacob is excited by his encounter with God. Fired-up by the meeting, Jacob seeks release for his zealous heart.

He has the audacity to start rolling a huge stone. A large rock, meant to last. A stone worthy of the weighty words Jacob heard from God that tipped the scales in his life, declaring Jacob a winner. Jacob forces the stone to stand up, like a pillar.

Lord, Jacob commemorated Your words with a stone pillar. I mark Your words with a flower, a satin ribbon, or a white-lace cross. Mark me as Your disciple. Stain me with Your blood. Be evident in me. I don't want Your word to remain stored on sacred pages where I encountered them. I want to set Your word loose in my life, in my world. Let me become a living memorial to You, preaching Your message with chutzpah, through Holy Spirit empowered deeds. Amen.

Anointed
Holy Chutzpah

"Take us to the supermarket to buy olive oil; my husband will bless it," Habona said to me. "John will anoint the four corners of the land where you will build the house of prayer."

John grew up in extreme poverty in the bush in Kenya. One day he listened to "Crazy Mary" who preached the gospel standing on a rock in his village. He took up the challenge and eventually joined Youth With A Mission, becoming the head of East Africa. John experienced God's anointing.

John had the bottle of oil in hand as we stood in a circle on the vacant Long Island property. John prayed over the golden liquid. Ed, Habona, and I responded, "Amen."

The oil looked unchanged, but 5'6" John appeared physically transformed after calling on the Lord.

His dark eyes flashed with holy purpose. A sacred tension filled his body. He clutched the bottle in his hand and lunged forward ignoring the scrub, heading for a corner of the land. We hurried behind him.

Bending on his knees he poured out oil, "I consecrate this property to the Lord's purposes. Holy unto God. Set apart for God's use. Guarded and kept by the heavenly host."

"Amen." We agreed.

"Take me to the next corner," he ordered.

Ed led us, cutting back tangles of wild rose stalks and raspberry canes, saving our pant legs and jackets from their thorns. We climbed over limbs and skirted tree trunks until Ed found the next survey marker.

Again, John knelt. The oil soaked into the ground. He prayed with power. "This land is holy to the Lord!"

For ages, people have boldly declared property to be holy to God by anointing it with oil. (Exodus 40:9) Nearly four thousand years ago God appeared to Jacob in Bethel. Afterwards, Jacob set up a stone pillar, "...to mark the place where God had spoken to him. He then poured wine over it as an offering to God and anointed the pillar with olive oil." (Genesis 35:14) His action declared the area holy.

Holy Spirit, anoint me with Holy Chutzpah. *Set me apart for Your special use. I dedicate myself to You. Show me visions of Your presence over neighborhoods and nations. Lead me to intercede. Teach me to anoint the corners of the continents in prayer. Show me how to declare the earth holy ground. You created the world and all that is in it for Your sacred purpose. Amen.*

Avoiding Pitfalls

"Step away from the pit," the congregation chorused back to me. I was teaching at a New York mission that supplies the destitute with physical and spiritual food.

"When you're walking down the street, every kind of enticement vies for your attention," I said. "Don't let distractions draw you into Satan's pit! When subway doors close, do you hear a computer-generated voice blare, 'Please, stand back. Please, stand back.'?"

"Yes!"

"If we listen with our hearts we will hear the Holy Spirit saying, 'Step away from the pit!' Warning bells ring in our minds signaling danger."

We can avoid serious pitfalls if we exercise caution. Too bad Jacob's son Joseph did not memorize the caution *step away from the pit*. He bragged about his dreams in which he had an exalted place among his brothers. After Joseph related his first dream, "...they hated him all the more because of his talk about his dreams." (Genesis 37:8)

Joseph didn't recognize his pride as a trap. He boasted about his next dream, further deteriorating family relationships. "So his brothers were wrought up against him... ." (Genesis 37:11) If he had not bragged about his dreams of fame, he may have averted his brothers' retaliation. As it was, they ganged up against him.

"'Here comes that dreamer,' they exclaimed. 'Come on, let's kill him and throw him into a deep pit... .'" (Genesis 37:19-20a)

Hellish chutzpah at work, a quick sketch of Satan's plan. He persists in urging us into temptation. If we cooperate with the devil and step into the pit he will not need to exert any more effort. We will rot over time. Fortunately, we escape the pit through repentance. The Blood of Jesus lifts us from despair.

As the story unfolds, God rescues Joseph and brings him through many purifying trials. Joseph matures into *holy chutzpah*. He rises to the second most powerful position in the land. Yet, he demonstrates uncompromising humility and audacious forgiveness, two characteristics rarely attributed to exceptionally rich and unconditionally powerful people. Joseph holds himself to the strictest standards of obedience and submission to God's word.

Still, I wonder. What if Joseph had displayed *holy chutzpah* earlier in his life? What if he had restrained his tongue? What if he had resisted temptations of pride and of provoking others to jealousy? Speculating on the possibilities increases my determination to step away from the pit.

~❧~

Lord, help me to listen and obey. I know You always warn me, but sometimes I plunge headlong into the pit. Please cultivate Holy Chutzpah *in me. I want a holy determination to step away from the pit. Thank You for merciful restoration and Your guidance that warns me of Satan's trap. Amen.*

God Promotes

I was fed up. Our Israeli tour bus had barely parked and the *pshsh* of the pneumatic brakes continued as they released air. Already she stood up from her front seat, waving to her group of friends. "I'll run ahead and get us the *best* places."

On our first day she fussed until the tour guide permanently reserved the front seat for her. Three times a day, for five days, I watched the same scenario reenacted. She ran ahead of everyone and held ten spots.

Meanwhile, Ed and I sat at the back of the bus and brought up the rear of every line.

"Let's hurry so we can get a good view," I said to Ed. I inhaled the dusty scent of the air as we made our way to the front of the mob of tourists.

I felt a prick in my conscience. I felt ashamed and slowed my pace. "God just reminded me," I said to

Ed. "He's the one who makes a place for us." We walked at a tranquil pace while five busloads of people barged past us. When we entered the church, there was not one seat left.

We stood at the back. My body was uncomfortable, but my soul was at total peace.

The preacher spoke for about ten minutes then he came to a stop. Upholstered chairs stood to his left and right.

"You folks in the back, come sit up front."

I walked up the aisle with Ed as though in a trance. God moved us from the back of the church to a seat of honor in the front and I was stunned. Imagine how Joseph felt when God moved him from a dank prison cell to prime minister of Egypt.

"'Who could do it better than Joseph? For he is a man obviously filled with the spirit of God... I hereby appoint you to direct this project... .'" (Genesis 41:38-40) God promoted Joseph. He had nothing to say on his own behalf that could have convinced the supreme ruler to appoint a prisoner as his right hand man. Joseph knew he had to rely on God to elevate him.

Holy chutzpah does not mean forging ahead with human determination, but clinging determinedly to God's Word regardless of our circumstances.

Lord, may I never promote myself. You alone deserve honor. Show me how to best exalt You. I want to be in the center of Your will. Please let me dwell there forever. Amen.

Ingenious
Holy Chutzpah

When Ed pulled an oval-shaped basket from the carton I caught my breath. "A Moses basket!" I said.

Geometric designs, reminiscent of Egypt, graced the sides. A Bangladeshi woman wove the cradle-like basket from cane, an abundant material in her country.

She works in a cooperative established by a non-governmental agency. They assist families with a per capita income of less than $50 a year to produce crafts.

Political turmoil and devastating storms have plagued Bangladesh. The resourceful weaver found a way to survive the grueling conditions in her land.

Moses' mother, Jochebed, would identify with the suffering woman who weaves her hopes into a basket. Jochebed was pregnant when a cruel edict hung over her people. Pharaoh's command reeked of hellish chutzpah. "...Pharoah gave this order to all of his people: 'Throw all the newborn Israelite boys into the Nile River... .'" (Exodus 1:22)

Expectant Jochebed kept her wits about her. After delivering her son Moses, she hid him. Imagine her terror. Pharaoh's edict commanded every Egyptian, not just soldiers, to execute Israelite boys. How often did Jochebed hear anguished screams from an Israelite mother who watched her baby drown? Jochebed's shrewdness would be Moses' salvation.

As her child grew it became more difficult to conceal him. When he reached three months of age, it became impossible. Jochebed developed an ingenious plan.

Egyptians built their boats with papyrus reeds that grew up to sixteen feet and flourished in marshes along the Nile. They sealed their vessels with pitch. Jochebed waterproofed a papyrus basket using tar and pitch.

She knew her basket would be seaworthy.

The new mother tenderly placed her small son in the little boat and set it among the tall reeds. She saved her boy's life through her inventiveness coupled with *holy chutzpah* to implement her plan.

Ingenious Holy Chutzpah

Lord, sometimes I have creative ideas, but lack Holy Chutzpah *to bring them to fruition. Dreams are not enough.*

I need to seek wise mentors, draw up a timetable, develop skills and set the project in motion. Your gutsy people bring You glory. I want to be counted among them. Amen.

Holy Chutzpah to Effect Change

A drunk driver caused the head-on collision and I was hospitalized in Rhode Island. My family arrived from New York.

Hospital rules prohibited overnight guests during the seventies, a policy that has relaxed through the years. I had just turned nineteen, but my mother still saw me as her baby.

She left her hotel room in the middle of the night. Exiting the hospital elevator, she crouched down and crept by the nurses' station undetected. Slipping into my room, she spent the night on the floor next to my bed. She considered it necessary to be available to care for me personally. And I needed her. She found a way to be close to her baby, and Jochebed found a way to be close to her Moses.

Holy Chutzpah to Effect Change

When the Egyptian princess scooped Moses from the Nile, his sister was nearby. She approached the royal lady, offering to find a wet-nurse for the infant. "Yes, do!" she agreed. Jochebed appeared.

"Take this child home and nurse him for me," the princess told her.

When the Hebrew woman would have stretched out her arms to receive her son, how did she hide her trembling? "So the baby's mother took her baby home and nursed him." (Exodus 2:9b)

When Jochebed heard Egyptian soldiers tramp down her dirt road, did she clutch Moses to her breast? Did she fear an Egyptian woman might observe her love for the child and become suspicious? She coped with extraordinary daily tension to do what was right.

Pharaoh would have considered Jochebed's defiance brazen noncompliance. If the Egyptians detected Jochebed's secret, what price would the hard-hearted despot demand of her? The Israelite woman had considered the possibilities. She took deliberate risks. She was determined to face any consequence with *holy chutzpah*.

Lord, show me when rules need to be reevaluated. How can I help effect change? More difficult questions may involve civil disobedience. I must play my part in the repeal of ungodly laws. My responsibility is to speak out against inhumane institutional and governmental policies. May I use every opportunity to register my opinion, while praying for a turn-around. Amen.

Holy Chutzpah Action

Elaine, a shy widow, grandmother of four and my close friend, prayed long and often. One day she heard God say, "Feed my sheep." The powerful experience replayed in her mind for days. Finally, she made eight bologna and cheese sandwiches and drove to a less affluent suburban town. Her foot shook on the gas pedal as she mentally rehearsed her plan. *"How will I ever do this?"*

She sighted a rough-looking man digging through a dumpster. Grandma Elaine pulled alongside the curb and rolled down her window. Mustering bravado she called, "Could you use a sandwich?" She pulled her head into her shoulders, like a turtle retreating into its shell, waiting for the reply. The man looked at her and nodded. She threw the sandwich out the window, gunned the engine and sped away thinking, *"Seven more to go, will I survive it?"* It took her three days to give all the sandwiches away.

Today, her feeding program provides meat, vegetables, sandwiches, and more to fifteen hundred hungry people weekly. Despite her timidity, she found *holy chutzpah* to act. If Elaine lived in Moses' generation I think they would have been buddies.

Moses encountered God in a flaming bush that didn't burn. He heard God's voice, he hid his face. (Exodus 3:2-10) Trembling with fear, Moses gave in to the Lord's command. He trudged off to Egypt, each step drawing him closer to a face-off with Pharaoh, a murderous dictator. At night when he stopped to rest in the wilderness by a crackling campfire, did Moses look into the flames and see again the burning bush? When he wrapped his cloak about himself and lay down, did he fall into an exhausted sleep while God's voice echoed through his dreams? Did Pharaoh's scowling face loom menacingly before him in the night hours? Whether Moses had consoling dreams or nightmares, he went forward with *holy chutzpah* and the Israelites went free, because he found courage to move in what he knew, leaving the unknown to God.

Holy Chutzpah Action

Lord, when I hear You, give me Holy Chutzpah *to act on what I hear. Let Your voice be enough for me, may I stop seeking guarantees. Help me take the first tentative step into the unknown. Set me free of the need to feel like I'm in control. I want to risk going forward in You, even if I don't know where it will lead me! I want You to be my compass. I want to rely on You for everything. Amen.*

Insistent
Holy Chutzpah

Elsa's Scandinavian accent enchanted me as I listened to her story while at the house of a mutual friend. Though she's spent a lifetime in the United States her inflection confirmed her heritage, as did her high cheekbones and delicate complexion.

Widowed at an early age with children to support, she asked God, "What can I do?" She found work in Manhattan. In the early morning she passed cardboard boxes on Lexington Avenue where street people had spent the night. She started making sandwiches for them. "We never wore sneakers to the office in those days, always high heels. The people heard my clicking heels and their hands rose up from the boxes. I put a sandwich in each hand. Not once did we see each other's faces.

"One day, I saw a woman badly beaten. She seemed out of her mind. Her accent was Scandinavian. I questioned her and she told me where she had been born.

"I called her embassy and told them the situation saying, 'You have to take care of her.' The embassy receptionist said, 'That is not our business.' 'Oh yes, it is. She is a citizen of your nation. And you have plenty of money. It's your responsibility to take care of her.'" Elsa persisted and argued with various embassy officials.

"The next day, I found they had sent an ambulance, taken her to a hospital, and then to a nursing home." Holy insistence yields results! A lesson we learn from Elsa and from Moses.

"'...Let My people go... .'" (Exodus 5:1) Moses delivered God's word to stubborn Pharaoh. Pharaoh refused to hear Moses' plea on behalf of the people, slaves who had no voice. Undaunted, Moses returned again and again to Pharaoh's court. As God's spokesman, he insisted "'...Let My people go... .'"

Intrepid Moses banged on the palace gates, made his way into the inner court and appeared before Pharaoh's throne. Other times he intercepted Pharaoh at the riverbank. Moses could have been executed! Yet, God was with Moses and his holy insistence yielded results. The people of Israel were set free.

Lord, may I insist on righteousness with Holy Chutzpah as Your servants Elsa and Moses demonstrated. I am inspired by their sanctified boldness, their persistent demands for justice. Use me, Lord, to speak for those who have been silenced by fear, hopelessness, and poverty. Teach me to obediently persevere according to Your Word, insisting on action from those who have the capacity to help the disempowered. Amen.

Holy Chutzpah
Meets the Challenge

Tears rolled down her smooth black cheeks as she told her story. Stella struggled to earn fees to attend school in Uganda, even though at that time she was a young teenager. She worked as a domestic—meaning she hauled firewood, chopped it, stacked it in the outdoor stove, prepared meals from chickens she slaughtered and from vegetables she carried on her head from the market.

Two years later she had earned enough to attend one year of school. While studying, she continued to work to save for the next semester. Her grades reflected her exhaustion. She began to fail. She had capacity but not means. After graduation, she despaired of attaining her business degree. She called out to God. Disheartened, she determined to lose herself in

Kampala the capital city and sever her village relationships. Stella was hard-pressed to hold on.

Simultaneously, Bridge for Peace heard God's challenging call to sponsor African students. Bridge for Peace (www.bridgeforpeace.org) is a non-profit ministry Ed and I began in 1988 to bring healing to the nations through Jesus Christ. Bridge for Peace had grown to an international ministry, but we had no experience in sponsoring students. What we had was a desire to obey God, a willingness to go where God led, and a determination to trust Him.

It took faith and time to raise funds. Stella had been a translator for one of our mission teams and had impressed all of the team members. We were not aware of her situation, but selected her as among the first to receive school fees. On a subsequent team visit to Africa she shared her experience with us.

"When I was told I would be sponsored, I couldn't believe it. I telephoned the program administrator and asked, 'Could you repeat what you said?' He did repeat it. It was true, I had a sponsor. I sat down and cried. I cried and cried and cried."

Stella had asked God's help, and God moved Bridge for Peace to bless Ugandan students. Bridge for Peace responded with joy, but how would we raise the funds? We soon experienced an outpouring of generosity—some of it from unusual sources. The Bible shows this in Exodus 12:35-36.

The children of Israel prepared to leave Egypt. They had flocks and herds, kneading bowls and unleavened dough, and little else. Obeying God, the Israelites "had asked from the Egyptians articles of silver, articles of gold, and clothing. And the Lord had given the people favor in the sight of the Egyptians, so that they granted them *what they requested.*"

It was unlikely the Egyptians would give anything to Israelites. It was equally unlikely Stella, living in remote Uganda, would receive sponsorship from the United States. However, nothing is impossible to God who moves men to meet the needs of people who have His favor.

⚜

Holy Spirit, stir me to hope and pray for Your provision to fulfill the big dreams You have given me. Like Stella, may prayer always be my first recourse. Grant me courage like the Israelites who knocked on hostile neighbors' doors in obedience to Your command, glorifying Your Name. Through my Holy Chutzpah *may You receive the honor You are due. Amen.*

Holy Chutzpah Risks

Marie and I sat side-by-side on the sandy beach, peering through our sunglasses at conical China Hat Island, a peak of green in the azure China Sea. She insisted Ed and I take a short break from our intense Philippine Island mission schedule and rest at her seaside home.

I asked about her family and she said, "My husband has gone to America with our son to open new markets for our products. We won't be together to celebrate our 25th anniversary, but he will call me from California. Our family will have a special cake for us, we will sing together and I will try not to cry, because I miss him very much."

The next week she told us God made her anniversary memorable with a special gift, but she needed *holy chutzpah* to receive it. This is what happened.

Marie wanted to show gratitude to God by helping someone else. "I purchased bags of groceries and accompanied my pastor and some church members to a remote island where the people have little. I distributed food to them. The church members were staying on the island for the weekend but I had to go home that evening, because my husband would be calling. By the time I got back to the dock the sun had set, a wind had sprung up, and the motor on the little skiff would not start. The water looked more threatening by the moment.

"My Pastor said, 'Marie, remain here with us!'

"'No pastor, I must speak with my husband tonight,' I said.

"Finally the engine turned over, but the skipper looked at the dark water and the clouds above and shook his head. He would not risk launching into a black sea. I closed my eyes and prayed. I told God of my longing to hear my husband's and son's voices and to celebrate with my family. When I opened my eyes, a glimmer of light had touched the crest of the waves. We looked up. Angry clouds parted like a curtain and pure white light shone from a full moon like a lantern in the sky. The skipper nodded and reached for the ropes.

"My hands shook with fear when I stepped into his boat. The waters looked very threatening. He pushed off and the little craft shuddered as we started for home. I heard my church family singing prayers from the shore behind.

"I made it back and drove to my mother's home where everyone was gathering for the anniversary party. I arrived to the arms of my loving family just as the phone rang. It was my husband. I was right on time! God provided the moonlight that took me across the sea."

Marie's story reminds me of another night when God showed His mastery of light and cloud and water. God's people journeyed from Israel in obedience to His command. "And the Lord went before them by day in a pillar of cloud to lead the way, and by night in a pillar of fire to give them light." (Exodus 13:21)

The Lord showed His sovereignty when the Israelites could not proceed without miraculous intervention. He lit the rocky wasteland with fire at night. The light protected them from predators, both of Egyptian soldiers and savage animals, which stalked victims in the darkness. God even rolled back the sea for the Israelites so they could pass on dry ground. (Exodus 14:21).

Sovreign Lord, Your timing is always optimal. I am determined to rely on You, not circumstances. Even when the situation seems risky, when You say the time is now, I want to launch out. When your servants obey, You move the very elements of the earth to ensure success. May I have Holy Chutzpah *to move with bold confidence in You and see Your power displayed in the world. Amen.*

Foundation for Healing Bible Study and Companion DVD

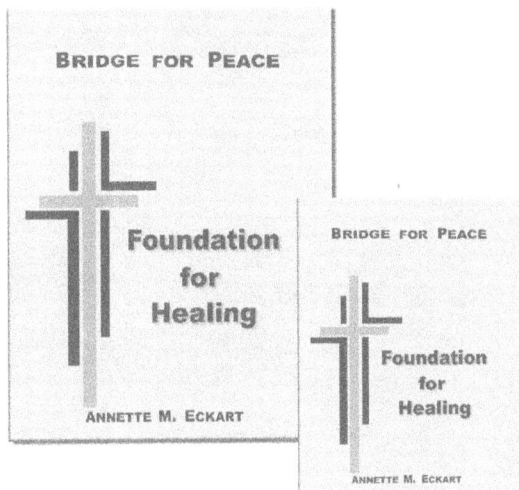

Foundation for Healing Bible Study is the fruit of 20 years of Annette Eckart's ministering healing in the Name of Jesus Christ. Learn and grow as you respond to questions that explore scripture and invite you to reflect on your experience. Read about miracles today in this 12 week Bible study.

The 4 hour Companion DVD is conveniently divided into 12 titles that can be shown weekly before the Bible study group. Each title has 20 minutes of Annette Eckart's dynamic teaching. This DVD is an invaluable tool to maximize your study experience.

To order:

Foundation for Healing Bible Study and DVD call Bridge for Peace 631-730-3982 or visit our website *www.bridgeforpeace.org*

www.ingramcontent.com/pod-product-compliance
Lightning Source LLC
Chambersburg PA
CBHW070827100426
42813CB00003B/514